TO

....

FROM

....

DATE

....

As we grow in our capacities to see and enjoy the joys that God has placed in our lives, life becomes a glorious experience of discovering His endless wonders.

*Delight yourself in the Lord
and he will give you the desires of your heart.*

Psalm 37:4 niv

> *Look deep within yourself and recognize what brings life and grace into your heart. It is this that can be shared with those around you. You are loved by God. This is an inspiration to love.*
>
> — CHRISTOPHER DE VINCK

May you have the power to understand, as all God's people should, how wide, how long, how high, and how deep his love is.

EPHESIANS 3:18 NLT

> *You are God's created beauty and the focus of His affection and delight.*
>
> — JANET L. SMITH

> *What great love the Father has lavished on us, that we should be called children of God!*
>
> 1 JOHN 3:1 NIV

> Women of adventure have conquered their fates and know how to live exciting and fulfilling lives right where they are. They have learned to reinvent themselves and find creative ways to enjoy the world and their place in it. They know how to take mini-vacations, stop and smell the roses, and live fully in the moment.
>
> — Barbara Jenkins

May the patience and encouragement that come from God allow you to live in harmony with each other.

ROMANS 15:5 NCV

> *I have never been a millionaire. But I have enjoyed a crackling fire, a glorious sunset, a walk with a friend, and a hug from a child. There are plenty of life's tiny delights for all of us.*
>
> — JACK ANTHONY

You're blessed when you're content with just who you are—no more, no less. That's the moment you find yourselves proud owners of everything that can't be bought.

MATTHEW 5:5 MSG

> *To love by freely giving is its own reward. To be possessed by love and to in turn give love away is to find the secret of abundant life.*
>
> — GLORIA GAITHER

I have come that they may have life, and that they may have it more abundantly.

JOHN 10:10 NKJV

Within each of us, just waiting to blossom,
is the wonderful promise of all we can be.

Clothe yourselves...with the beauty that comes from within, the unfading beauty of a gentle and quiet spirit, which is so precious to God.

1 Peter 3:4 nlt

> *O*ur God is so wonderfully good, and lovely,
> and blessed in every way that the mere fact of belonging
> to Him is enough for an untellable fullness of joy!
>
> — HANNAH WHITALL SMITH

*Worship the LORD with gladness;
come before him with joyful songs.*

PSALM 100:2 NIV

The wonder of living is held within the beauty of silence, the glory of sunlight...the sweetness of fresh spring air, the quiet strength of earth, and the love that lies at the very root of all things.

The Lord *is my shepherd, I shall not want.*
He makes me lie down in green pastures;
He leads me beside quiet waters.
He restores my soul.

Psalm 23:1–3 nasb

> *E*very person ever created is so special that their presence in the world makes it richer and fuller and more wonderful than it could ever have been without them.

God has given each of you a gift from his great variety of spiritual gifts. Use them well to serve one another.

1 Peter 4:10 NLT

Each day is a treasure box of gifts from God, just waiting to be opened. Open your gifts with excitement. You will find forgiveness attached to ribbons of joy. You will find love wrapped in sparkling gems.

— JOAN CLAYTON

Happy are those who hear the joyful call to worship, for they will walk in the light of your presence, LORD.

PSALM 89:15 NLT

> *Everything in life is most fundamentally a gift.*
> *And you receive it best, and you live it best,*
> *by holding it with very open hands.*
>
> — Leo O'Donovan

Every good gift and every perfect gift is from above, and comes down from the Father of lights, with whom there is no variation or shadow of turning.

JAMES 1:17 NKJV

> *You have a unique message to deliver, a unique song to sing, a unique act of love to bestow. This message, this song, and this act of love have been entrusted exclusively to the one and only you.*
>
> — John Powell

> *May Jesus himself and God our Father, who reached out in love and surprised you with gifts of unending help and confidence, put a fresh heart in you, invigorate your work, enliven your speech.*
>
> 2 Thessalonians 2:16–17 MSG

> *Joy is...deeper than an emotional expression of happiness.
> Joy is a growing, evolving manifestation of
> God in my life as I walk with Him.*
>
> — BONNIE MONSON

Though you have not seen Him, you love Him, and though you do not see Him now, but believe in Him, you greatly rejoice with joy inexpressible.

1 Peter 1:8 nasb

> God made you so you could share in His creation,
> could love and laugh and know Him.
>
> — TED GRIFFEN

Whoever loves God is known by God.

1 Corinthians 8:3 niv

> The place where God calls you to is the place where your deep gladness and the world's deep hunger meet.
>
> — FREDERICK BUECHNER

> *Blessed are those who hunger and thirst for righteousness, for they shall be satisfied.*
>
> MATTHEW 5:6 NASB

> Are you aware that the Father takes delight in you and that He thinks about you all the time?
>
> — JACK FROST

The LORD your God is with you.... He will take great delight in you, he will quiet you with his love, he will rejoice over you with singing.

ZEPHANIAH 3:17 NIV

> The God who created, names, and numbers the stars
> in the heavens also numbers the hairs of my head.... He pays attention
> to very big things and to very small ones. What matters to me
> matters to Him, and that changes my life.
>
> — Elisabeth Elliot

> *What is the price of five sparrows—two copper coins? Yet God does not forget a single one of them. And the very hairs on your head are all numbered. So don't be afraid; you are more valuable to God than a whole flock of sparrows.*
>
> Luke 12:6–7 NLT

*S*ome days, it is enough encouragement just to watch the clouds break up and disappear, leaving behind a blue patch of sky and bright sunshine that is so warm upon my face. It's a glimpse of divinity; a kiss from heaven.

> *Dear friend, I pray that you may enjoy good health and that all may go well with you, even as your soul is getting along well.*
>
> 3 JOHN 1:2 NIV

> Work is fine, but when it's mixed with fun it's a lot better. Don't be a fun pauper. Get into the delights a good God has put into the world.
>
> — NORMAN VINCENT PEALE

*Happy are those who respect the Lord and obey him.
You will enjoy what you work for,
and you will be blessed with good things.*

PSALM 128:1–2 NCV

> *O*ur true places as women in God's Story
> are as diverse and unique as wildflowers in a field.
>
> — JOHN AND STASI ELDREDGE

It is clear to us, friends, that God not only loves you very much but also has put His hand on you for something special.

1 Thessalonians 1:4 msg

> *D*ear Lord, grant me the grace of wonder. Surprise me,
> amaze me, awe me in every crevice of Your universe.
> Delight me to see how Your Christ plays in ten thousand places.
>
> — ABRAHAM JOSHUA HESCHEL

*The heavens declare the glory of God;
the skies proclaim the work of his hands.
Day after day they pour forth speech;
night after night they reveal knowledge.*

PSALM 19:1–2 NIV

God knows the rhythm of my spirit and knows my heart thoughts.
He is as close as breathing.

*I know the Lord is always with me.
I will not be shaken, for he is right beside me.
No wonder my heart is glad, and I rejoice.*

Psalm 16:8–9 NLT

> God came to us because God wanted to join us on the road,
> to listen to our story, and to help us realize that we are not walking
> in circles but moving toward the house of peace and joy.
>
> HENRI J. M. NOUWEN

Peace I leave with you, My peace I give to you; not as the world gives do I give to you. Let not your heart be troubled, neither let it be afraid.

JOHN 14:27 NKJV

*Tuck [this] thought into your heart today.
Treasure it. Your Father God cares about your daily
everythings that concern you.*

KAY ARTHUR

*I call on you, my God, for you will answer me;
turn your ear to me and hear my prayer.
Show me the wonders of your great love.*

Psalm 17:6–7 NIV

Experience God in the breathless wonder and startling beauty that is all around you. His sun shines warm upon your face.... Like the first rays of morning light, celebrate the start of each day with God.

WENDY MOORE

> *Because of God's tender mercy, the morning light from heaven is about to break upon us, to give light to those who sit in darkness… and to guide us to the path of peace.*
>
> LUKE 1:78–79 NLT

Take time to notice all the usually unnoticed, simple things in life. Delight in the never-ending hope that's available every day!

Rejoice always, pray without ceasing, in everything give thanks.
1 Thessalonians 5:16–18 NKJV

I delight in your unfailing love, God.
No matter where I go, it surrounds me.

Your love, Lord, reaches to the heavens, your faithfulness to the skies. Your righteousness is like the highest mountains, your justice like the great deep.... How priceless is your unfailing love, O God!

PSALM 36:5–7 NIV

> *Live for today but hold your hands open to tomorrow. Anticipate the future and its changes with joy. There is a seed of God's love in every event, every circumstance...in which you may find yourself.*
>
> — BARBARA JOHNSON

> God is the one who provides seed for the farmer and then bread to eat. In the same way, he will provide and increase your resources and then produce a great harvest of generosity in you.
>
> 2 Corinthians 9:10 NLT

> *Faith in God gives your life a center from which you can reach out and dare to love the world.*
>
> — BARBARA FARMER

> *Whoever believes in me, as Scripture has said, rivers of living water will flow from within them.*
>
> JOHN 7:38 NIV

> God's holy beauty comes near you, like a spiritual scent,
> and it stirs your drowsing soul.... He creates in you the desire to find Him...
> and to press peacefully against His heart wherever He is.
>
> JOHN OF THE CROSS

Keep company with me and you'll learn to live freely and lightly.

MATTHEW 11:30 MSG

> *Like supernatural effervescence, praise will sometimes bubble up from the joy of simply knowing Christ. Praise like that is...delight. Pure pleasure!*
>
> — JONI EARECKSON TADA

> *O*ur mouths were filled with laughter,
> our tongues with songs of joy....
> The Lord has done great things for us,
> and we are filled with joy.
>
> Psalm 126:2–3 niv

*The patterns of our days are always changing...
rearranging...and each design for living is unique...
graced with its own special beauty.*

*The Lord will work out His plans for my life—
for your faithful love, O Lord, endures forever.*

PSALM 138:8 NLT

Be still, and in the quiet moments, listen to the voice of your heavenly Father. His words can renew your spirit... no one knows you and your needs like He does.

JANET L. SMITH

> *God will supply all your needs according to His riches in glory in Christ Jesus.*
>
> PHILIPPIANS 4:19 NASB

The wind rushing through the grass, the thrush in the treetops, and children tumbling in senseless mirth stir in us a bright faith in life.

DONALD CULROSS PEATTIE

*Light in a messenger's eyes brings joy to the heart,
and good news gives health to the bones.*

PROVERBS 15:30 NIV

> *You can talk to God because God listens. Your voice matters in heaven. He takes you very seriously.... Even if you stammer or stumble, even if what you have to say impresses no one, it impresses God—and He listens.*
>
> —Max Lucado

*I prayed to the Lord, and He answered me.
He freed me from all my fears.
Those who look to Him for help will be radiant with joy.*

PSALM 34:4–5 NLT

> The moment you begin to delight in beauty,
> your heart and mind are raised.
>
> — BASIL HUME

> Whatever is true, whatever is honorable, whatever is right, whatever is pure, whatever is lovely, whatever is of good repute, if there is any excellence and if anything worthy of praise, dwell on these things.
>
> PHILIPPIANS 4:8 NASB

> Only He who created the wonders of the world entwines hearts in an eternal way.

> *He has made everything beautiful in its time.*
> *He has also set eternity in the human heart.*
>
> ECCLESIASTES 3:11 NIV

> The wonder of our Lord is that He is so accessible to us in the common things of our lives: the cup of water...welcoming children into our arms...fellowship over a meal...giving thanks.
>
> — NANCIE CARMICHAEL

> You make known to me the path of life;
> you will fill me with joy in your presence,
> with eternal pleasures at your right hand.
>
> PSALM 16:11 NIV

> Be such a person, and live such a life, that if every one were such as you, and every life a life such as yours, this earth would be God's paradise.
>
> — PHILLIPS BROOKS

> *Live out your God-created identity. Live generously and graciously toward others, the way God lives toward you.*
>
> MATTHEW 5:48 MSG

Loving Creator, help me reawaken my childlike sense of wonder at the delights of Your world!

— MARILYN MORGAN HELLEBERG

> *The God who made the whole world and everything in it is the Lord of the land and the sky.... This God is the One who gives life, breath, and everything else to people.*
>
> ACTS 17:24–25 NCV

> *Peace with God brings the peace of God. It is a peace that settles our nerves, fills our mind, floods our spirit, and in the midst of the uproar around us, gives us the assurance that everything is all right.*
>
> BOB MUMFORD

May the God of hope fill you with all joy and peace as you trust in him, so that you may overflow with hope.

ROMANS 15:13 NIV

A living, loving God can and does make His presence felt, can and does speak to us in the silence of our hearts, can and does warm and caress us till we no longer doubt that He is near, that He is here.

BRENNAN MANNING

Draw near to God and He will draw near to you.

JAMES 4:8 NASB

> *All [God's] glory and beauty come from within, and there He delights to dwell. His visits there are frequent, His conversation sweet, His comforts refreshing, His peace passing all understanding.*
>
> — THOMAS À KEMPIS

The peace of God, which surpasses all understanding, will guard your hearts and minds through Christ Jesus.

PHILIPPIANS 4:7 NKJV

He is the Source. Of everything. Strength for your day. Wisdom for your task. Comfort for your soul. Grace for your battle. Provision for each need. Understanding for each failure. Assistance for every encounter.

JACK HAYFORD

I can do all this through him who gives me strength.

PHILIPPIANS 4:13 NIV

> *Just slipping quietly into the presence of God can be so exotic and fresh that it delights us enormously.*
>
> — RICHARD J. FOSTER

> *The one thing I ask of the LORD—the thing I seek most—
> is to live in the house of the LORD all the days of my life,
> delighting in the LORD's perfections and meditating in his Temple.*
>
> PSALM 27:4 NLT

A quiet morning with a loving God puts the events of the upcoming day into proper perspective.

JANETTE OKE

> *In the morning, L*ORD*, you hear my voice;*
> *in the morning I lay my requests before you*
> *and wait expectantly.*
>
> PSALM 5:3 NIV

> *Beauty puts a face on God. When we gaze at nature, at a loved one, at a work of art, our soul immediately recognizes and is drawn to the face of God.*
>
> — Margaret Brownley

*Let the beauty of the LORD our God be upon us,
And establish the work of our hands for us.*

PSALM 90:17 NKJV

> There is in every human being's heart the love of wonder,
> the sweet amazement at the stars and starlike things...the unfailing
> childlike appetite for what-next, and the joy of the game of living.
>
> SAMUEL ULLMAN

> *You have begun to live the new life, in which you are being made new and are becoming like the One who made you. This new life brings you the true knowledge of God.*
>
> COLOSSIANS 3:10 NCV

Have you ever thought that in every action of grace in your heart you have the whole omnipotence of God engaged to bless you?

ANDREW MURRAY

From his abundance we have all received one gracious blessing after another.

JOHN 1:16 NLT

*Only God gives true peace—a quiet gift
He sets within us just when we think
we've exhausted our search for it.*

*You will keep in perfect peace all who trust in you,
all whose thoughts are fixed on you!*

ISAIAH 26:3 NLT

> *I think what we're longing for is not "the good life" as it's been advertised to us...but life in its fullness, its richness, its abundance. Living more reflectively helps us enter into that fullness.*
>
> — KEN GIRE

> *I pray that out of his glorious riches he may strengthen you with power through his Spirit in your inner being.*
>
> Ephesians 3:16 NIV

> *True prayer is synonymous with gratitude and contentment....*
> *How marvelous prayer is for communicating our delight with God.*
>
> — GLORIA GAITHER

> *Bless the Lord, O my soul,*
> *And forget not all His benefits....*
> *Who crowns you with lovingkindness and tender mercies,*
> *Who satisfies your mouth with good things.*
>
> Psalm 103:2, 4–5

> *I am convinced that God has built into all of us an appreciation of beauty and has even allowed us to participate in the creation of beautiful things and places.*
>
> — MARY JANE WORDEN

> We ask God to give you...spiritual wisdom and understanding.
> Then the way you live will always honor and please the Lord,
> and your lives will produce every kind of good fruit.
>
> COLOSSIANS 1:9–10 NLT

> *The Lord gives you the experience of enjoying His presence. He touches you, and His touch is so delightful that, more than ever, you are drawn inwardly to Him.*
>
> — Madame Jeanne Guyon

*O Lord, you have examined my heart and know everything about me.
You know when I sit down or stand up. You know my thoughts even when I'm far away....
You go before me and follow me. You place your hand of blessing on my head.*

Psalm 139:1–2, 5 nlt

> *Slow down and enjoy life. It's not only the scenery you miss by going too fast—you also miss the sense of where you are going and why.*
>
> — EDDIE CANTOR

We know that all things work together for good to those who love God, to those who are the called according to His purpose.

ROMANS 8:28 NKJV

*That I am here is a wonderful mystery
to which I will respond with joy.*

*Satisfy us in the morning with your unfailing love,
that we may sing for joy and be glad all our days.*

PSALM 90:14 NIV

When we take time to notice the simple things in life, we never lack for encouragement. We discover we are surrounded by a limitless hope that's just wearing everyday clothes.

*Ears to hear and eyes to see—
both are gifts from the L*ORD.

PROVERBS 20:12 NLT

> *E*ach one of us is God's special work of art.
> Through us, He teaches and inspires, delights and encourages,
> informs and uplifts all those who view our lives.
>
> JONI EARECKSON TADA

You are the light of the world. A town built on a hill cannot be hidden. Neither do people light a lamp and put it under a bowl. Instead they put it on its stand, and it gives light to everyone in the house. In the same way, let your light shine before others, that they may see your good deeds and glorify your Father in heaven.

MATTHEW 5:14–16 NIV

> To desire to love God is to love to desire Him,
> and hence to love Him, for love is the root of all desire.
>
> — JEAN-PIERRE CAMUS

> *Whom have I in heaven but you? I desire you more than anything on earth. My health may fail, and my spirit may grow weak, but God remains the strength of my heart; he is mine forever.*
>
> Psalm 73:25–26 NLT

> *L*ove the moment, and the energy of that moment will spread beyond all boundaries.
>
> — CORITA KENT

The Lord will guide you always; He will satisfy your needs in a sun-scorched land and will strengthen your frame. You will be like a well-watered garden, like a spring whose waters never fail.

Isaiah 58:11 NIV

> *The secret of life is that all we have and are is a gift of grace to be shared.*
>
> — LLOYD JOHN OGILVIE

Love each other with genuine affection, and take delight in honoring each other.

ROMANS 12:10 NLT

> *I* still find each day too short for all the thoughts I want to think, all the walks I want to take, all the books I want to read, and all the friends I want to see. The longer I live, the more my mind dwells upon the beauty and the wonder of the world.
>
> — JOHN BURROUGHS

Many, O Lord my God, are the wonders which You have done, and Your thoughts toward us; there is none to compare with You.

Psalm 40:5 nasb

> [God] delights to meet the faith of one who looks up to Him and says, "Lord, You know that I cannot do this—but I believe that You can!"
>
> — AMY CARMICHAEL

> *He led me to a place of safety;*
> *he rescued me because he delights in me.*
>
> 2 SAMUEL 22:20 NLT

Time, indeed, is a sacred gift, and each day is a little life.

Sir John Lubbock

Take your everyday, ordinary life—your sleeping, eating, going-to-work, and walking-around life—and place it before God as an offering. Embracing what God does for you is the best thing you can do for him.

ROMANS 12:1 MSG

> *Isn't it splendid to think of all the things there are to find out about?*
> *It just makes me feel glad to be alive—it's such an interesting world.*
> *It wouldn't be half so interesting if we knew all about everything.*
>
> — Lucy Maud Montgomery

The whole earth is filled with awe at your wonders; where morning dawns, where evening fades, you call forth songs of joy.

PSALM 65:8 NIV

> *In ordinary life we hardly realize that we receive a great deal more than we give, and that it is only with gratitude that life becomes rich.*
>
> — DIETRICH BONHOEFFER

It is good to give thanks to the Lord and to sing praises to Your name, O Most High; to declare Your loving kindness in the morning and Your faithfulness by night.

Psalm 92:1–2 nasb

> At times it is only necessary to rest one's self in silence for a few minutes, in order to take off the pressure and become wonderfully refreshed.
>
> JOHN PAUL DRESSER

*Let all that I am wait quietly before God,
for my hope is in him.*

PSALM 62:5 NLT

> *God's quest to be glorified and our quest to be satisfied reach their goal in this one experience: our delight in God which overflows in praise.*
>
> — JOHN PIPER

Blessed are the people who know the joyful sound!
They walk, O Lord, in the light of Your countenance.
In Your name they rejoice all day long,
And in Your righteousness they are exalted.

Psalm 89:15–16 nkjv

> *How wonderful it is that nobody need wait a single moment before starting to improve the world.*
>
> — ANNE FRANK

*The generous will prosper;
those who refresh others will themselves be refreshed.*

PROVERBS 11:25 NLT

*T*oday is unique! It has never occurred before, and it will never be repeated. At midnight it will end, quietly, suddenly, totally. Forever. But the hours between now and then are opportunities with eternal possibilities.

CHARLES R. SWINDOLL

> *This is the day the LORD has made;*
> *We will rejoice and be glad in it.*
>
> PSALM 118:24 NKJV

Simply Ellie
Franklin, TN 37067
EllieClaire.com
Ellie Claire is a registered trademark of Worthy Media, Inc.

My Soul Finds Rest 978-1-63326-067-2; *Hope* 978-1-63326-071-9;
Sing to the Lord 978-1-63326-070-2; *Amazing Grace* 978-1-63326-069-6;
New Every Morning 978-1-63326-077-1; *Promises and Blessings for Your Heart* 978-1-63326-068-9;
For I Know the Plans 978-1-63326-073-3; *Delight Yourself in the Lord* 978-1-63326-075-7;
When God Thinks of You 978-1-63326-072-6; *Everything Beautiful* 978-1-63326-074-0;
Good Morning, God 978-1-63326-076-4; *My Gratitude Journal* 978-1-63326-078-8;
Whispers of Grace 978-1-63326-079-5; *Amazing Grace* 978-1-63326-081-8;
The Lord Is with You 978-1-63326-083-2; *Trust in the Lord* 978-1-63326-080-1;
For I Know the Plans 978-1-63326-082-5; *Be Still and Know* 978-1-63326-084-9

© 2015 by Simply Ellie
Published by Ellie Claire, an imprint of Worthy Publishing Group, a division of Worthy Media, Inc.

All rights reserved. No part of this book may be reproduced in any form without permission in writing from the publisher.

Scripture references are from the following sources: The Holy Bible, New International Version®, NIV®. Copyright © 1973, 1978, 1984, 2011 by Biblica, Inc.™ Used by permission of Zondervan. All rights reserved worldwide. The Holy Bible, New King James Version (NKJV). Copyright © 1982 by Thomas Nelson, Inc. Used by permission. The New American Standard Bible® (NASB), Copyright © 1960, 1962, 1963, 1968, 1971, 1972, 1973, 1975, 1977, 1995 by The Lockman Foundation. Used by permission. The Holy Bible, New Living Translation (NLT), copyright 1996, 2004. 2007 by Tyndale House Foundation. Used by permission of Tyndale House Publishers, Inc., Carol Stream, Illinois 60188. The Message (MSG). Copyright © 1993, 1994, 1995, 1996, 2000, 2001, 2002 by Eugene Peterson. Used by permission of NavPress, Colorado Springs, CO. The New Century Version® (NCV). Copyright © 1987, 1988, 1991, 2005 by Thomas Nelson, Inc. Used by permission. All rights reserved.

Excluding Scripture verses and deity pronouns, in some quotations references to men and masculine pronouns have been replaced with gender-neutral or feminine references. Additionally, in some quotations we have carefully updated verb forms and wording that may distract modern readers.

Stock or custom editions of Simply Ellie titles may be purchased in bulk for educational, business, ministry, fundraising, or sales promotional use. For information, please e-mail info@EllieClaire.com

Compiled by Barbara Farmer
Printed in China